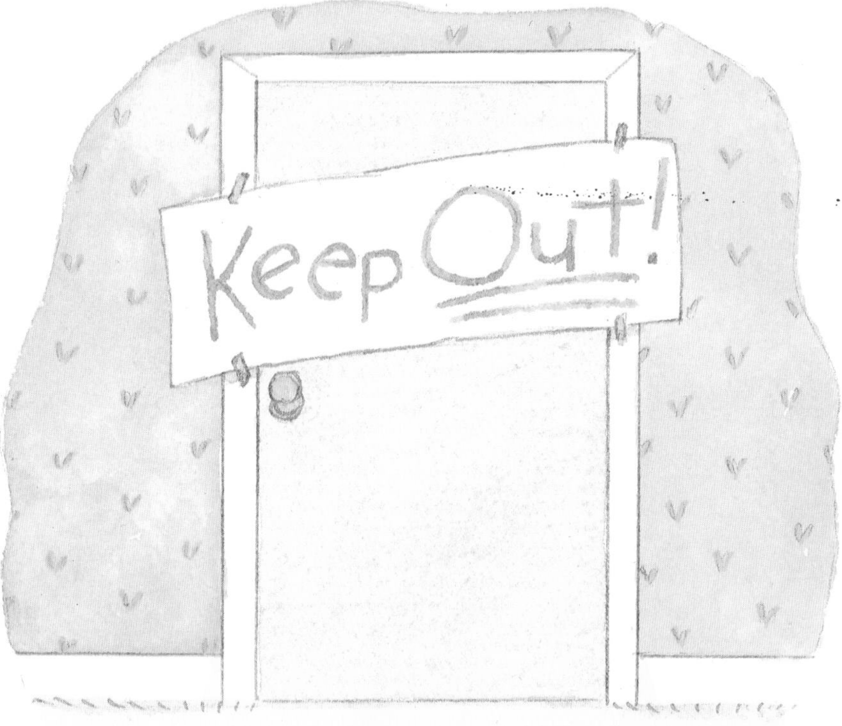

Written by Will Hardy
Illustrated by Marsha Winborn

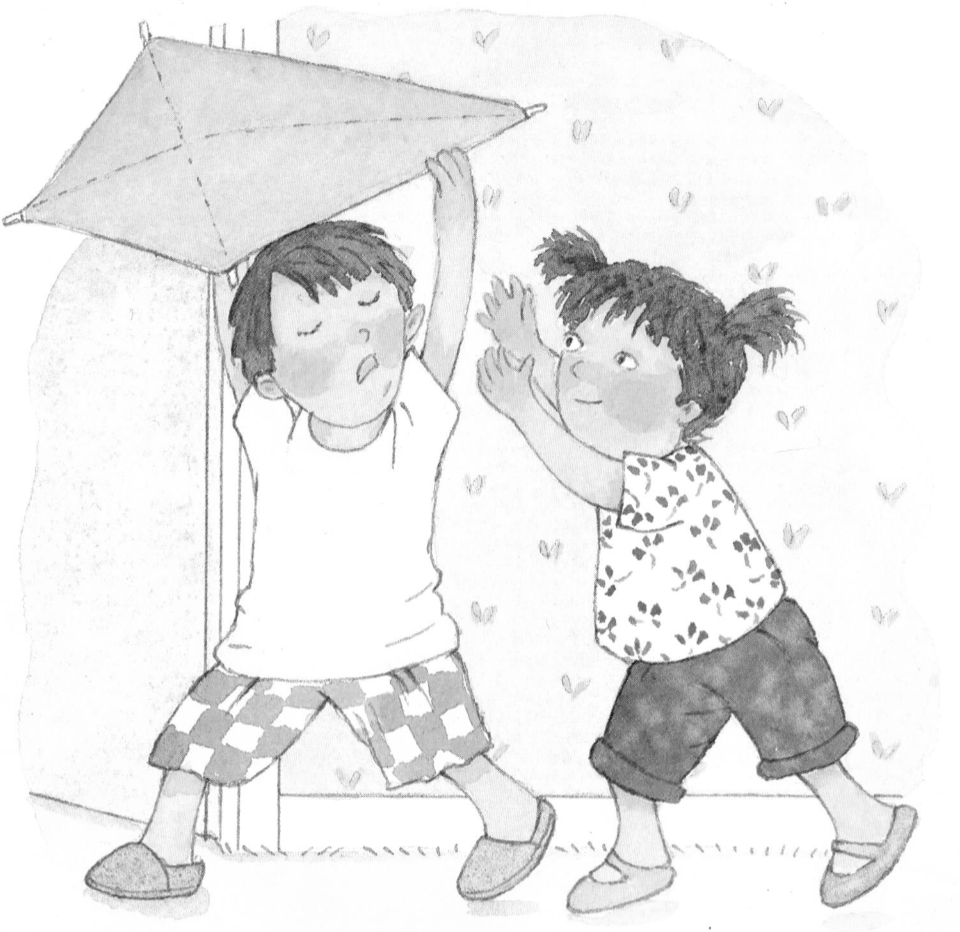

It is my kite.

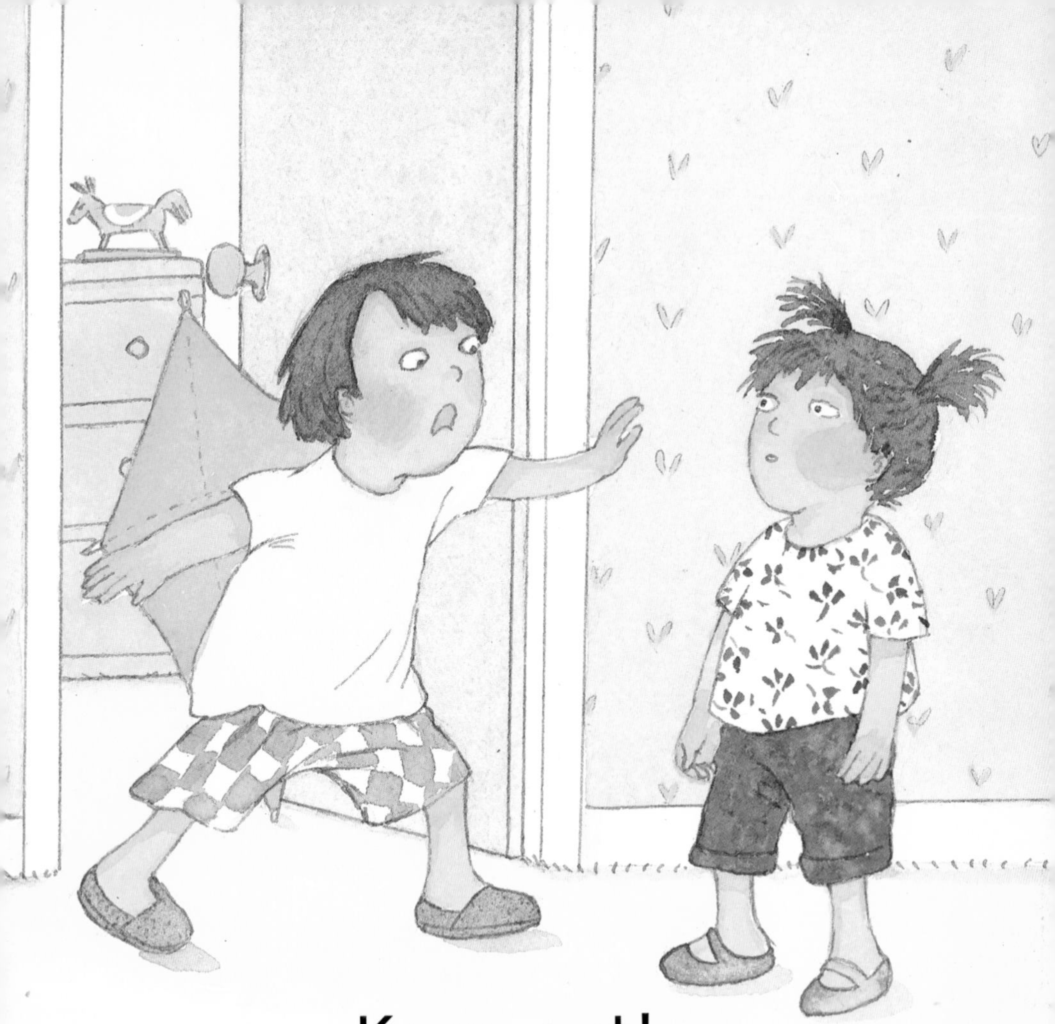

Keep out!

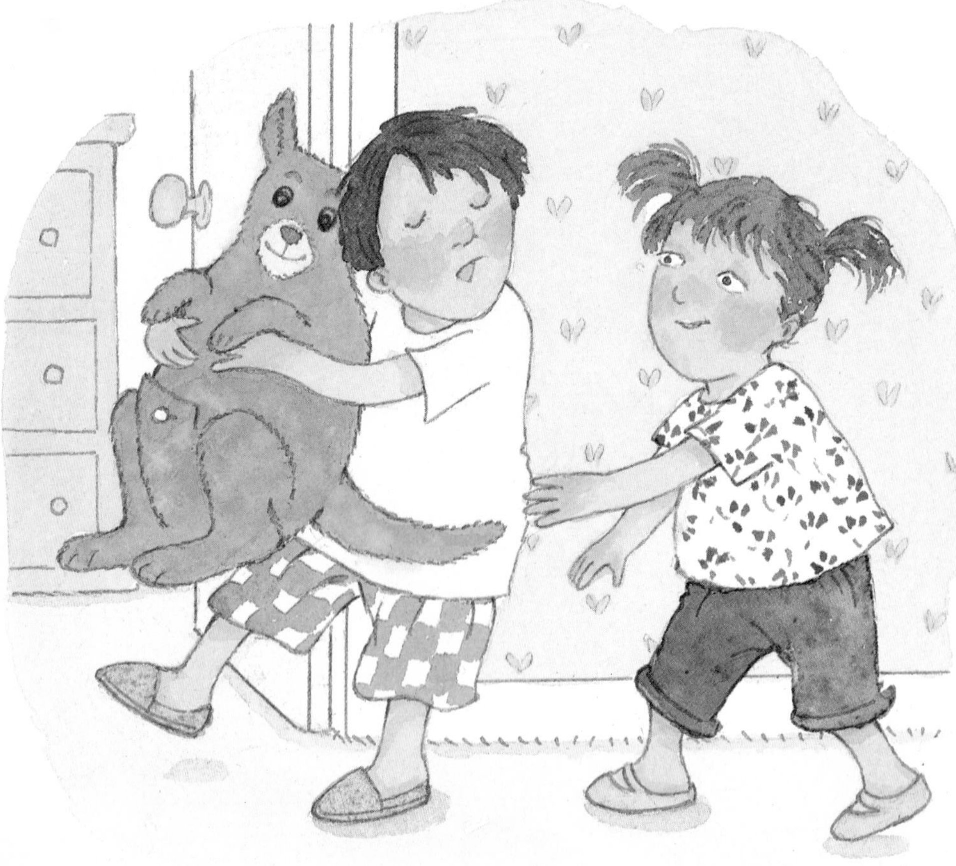

It is my kangaroo.

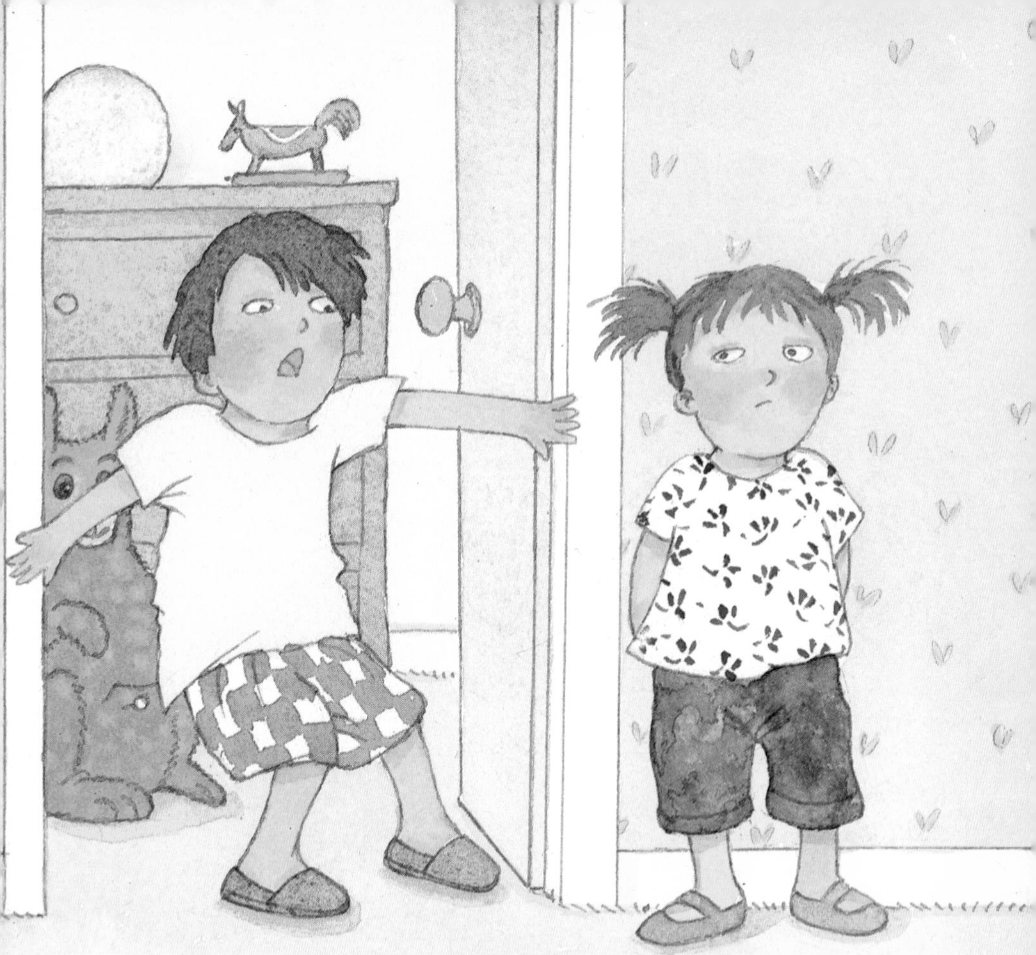

Keep out!

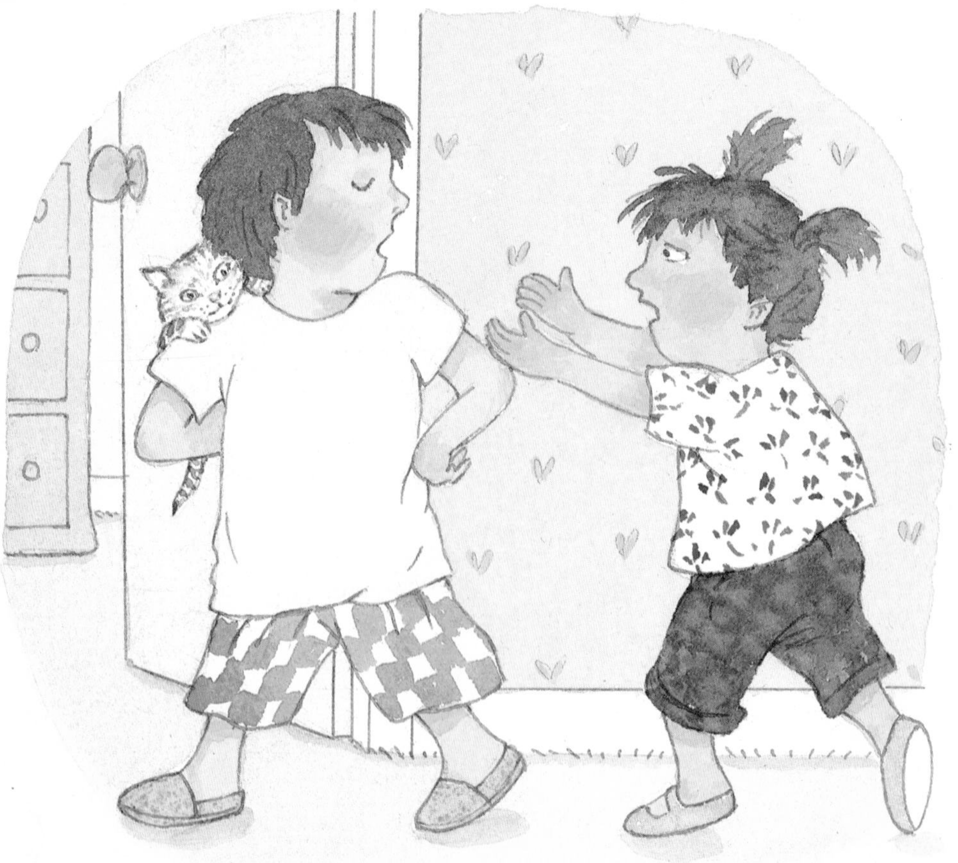

It is my kitten.

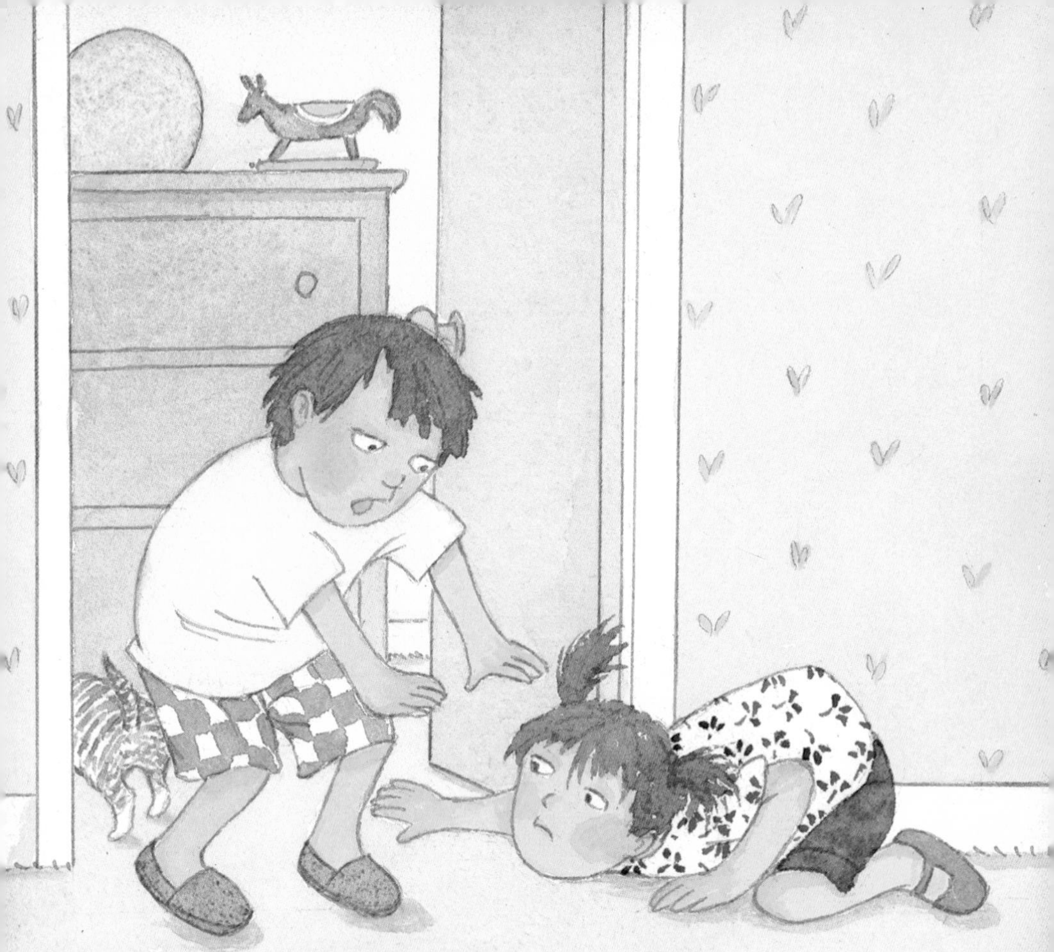

Keep out!

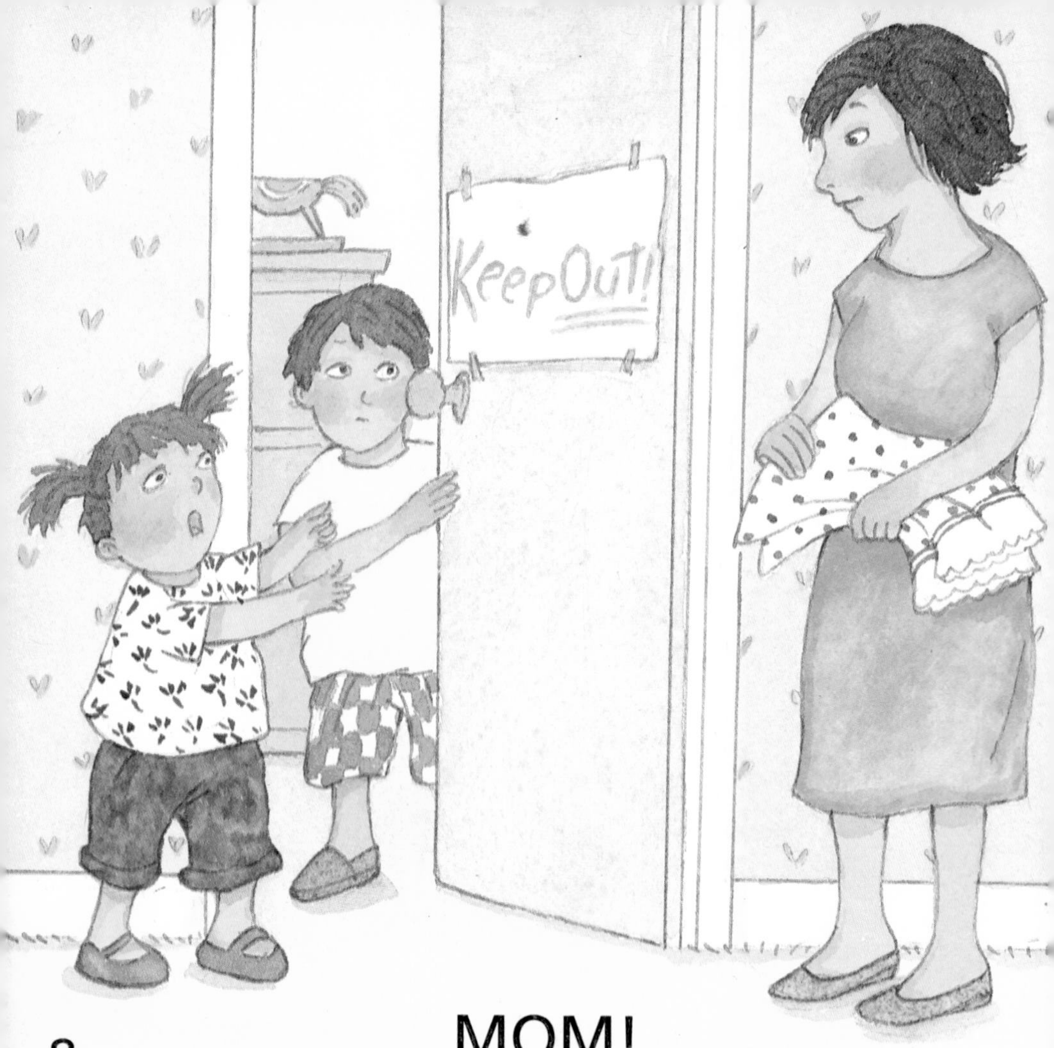

MOM!